A Guide for Using

Kira-Kira

in the Classroom

Based on the novel written by Cynthia Kadohata

This guide written by

Melissa Hart, M.F.A.

Teacher Created Resources, Inc.
6421 Industry Way
Westminster, CA 92683
www.teachercreated.com
©2006 Teacher Created Resources, Inc.
Made in U.S.A.
ISBN-1-4206-3003-2

Edited by
Sara Connolly

Illustrated by
Mark Mason

Cover Art by
Courtney Barnes

Table of Contents

Introduction

A good book can enrich our lives like a good friend. Fictional characters can inspire us and teach us about the world in which we live. We can turn to books for companionship, entertainment, and guidance. A truly beloved book may touch our lives forever.

Great care has been taken with Literature Units to select books that are sure to become your students' good friends!

Teachers who use this unit will find the following features to supplement their own ideas:

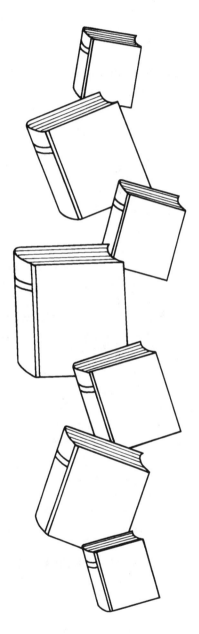

- Sample Lesson Plans

- Pre-Reading Activities

- A Biographical Sketch and Picture of the Author

- A Book Summary

- Vocabulary Lists and Suggested Vocabulary Activities

- Chapters grouped for study with each section including:

  — *quizzes*

  — *hands-on projects*

  — *cooperative learning activities*

  — *cross-curricular connections*

  — *extensions into the reader's life*

- Post-Reading Activities

- Book Report Ideas

- Research Activities

- Culminating Activities

- Three Different Options for Unit Tests

- Bibliography of Related Reading

- Answer Key

We are certain this unit will be a valuable addition to your own curriculum ideas to supplement *Kira-Kira.*

Sample Lesson Plans

The time it takes to complete the suggested lessons below will vary, depending on the type of activity, and your students' abilities and interest levels.

Lesson 1
- Introduce and complete some or all of the pre-reading activities from "Before Reading the Book." (page 5)
- Read "About the Author" with students. (page 6)
- Introduce the vocabulary list for Section 1. (page 8)

Lesson 2
- Read Chapters 1–3. As you read, place the vocabulary words in the context of the book and discuss their meanings.
- Locate Iowa on the classroom map. Then locate Georgia. Katie and her family travel from Iowa to Georgia in Section 1 of this novel.
- Chose a vocabulary activity to complete. (page 9)
- Complete "Making Rice Balls." (page 11)
- Learn to play chess. (page 12)
- Learn about the 1950s. (page 13)
- Keep a diary. (page 14)
- Administer the Section 1 Quiz. (page 10)
- Introduce the vocabulary list for Section 2. (page 8)

Lesson 3
- Read Chapters 4–6. As you read, place the vocabulary words in the context of the book and discuss their meanings.
- Choose a vocabulary activity to complete. (page 9)
- Write a short story. (page 16)
- Learn to go camping. (page 17)
- Play Dodgeball. (page 18)
- Make selfish and unselfish wishes. (page 19)
- Administer the Section 2 Quiz. (page 15)
- Introduce the vocabulary list for Section 3. (page 8)

Lesson 4
- Read Chapters 7–9. As you read, place the vocabulary words in the context of the book and discuss their meanings.
- Choose a vocabulary activity to complete. (page 9)
- Revisit The Ed Sullivan Show. (page 21)

- Learn about unions. (page 22)
- Play Scrabble. (page 23)
- Explore being sick. (page 24)
- Administer the Section 3 Quiz. (page 20)
- Introduce the vocabulary list for Section 4. (page 8)

Lesson 5
- Read Chapters 10–12. As you read, place the vocabulary words in the context of the book and discuss their meanings.
- Choose a vocabulary activity to complete. (page 9)
- Make an ocean diorama. (page 26)
- Learn about chickens. (page 27)
- Make scientific observations in squares (page 28)
- Explore themes. (page 29)
- Administer the Section 4 Quiz. (page 25)
- Introduce the vocabulary list for Section 5. (page 8)

Lesson 6
- Read Chapters 13–15. As you read, place the vocabulary words in the context of the book and discuss their meanings.
- Choose a vocabulary activity to complete. (page 9)
- Make constellations. (page 31)
- Listen to your world. (page 32)
- Travel through the U.S. (page 33)
- Learn about grief. (page 34)
- Administer the Section 5 Quiz. (page 30)

Lesson 7
- Discuss questions students have about the book. (page 35)
- Assign a book report and research activity. (pages 36–37)
- Begin work on one or more culminating activities. (pages 39–42)

Lesson 8
- Choose and administer Unit Tests: 1, 2, and/or 3. (pages 43–45)
- Discuss students' feelings about the book.
- Provide a bibliography of related reading. (page 46)

4

Before the Book

Before you begin reading *Kira-Kira* with your students, complete one or more of the following pre-reading activities to stimulate their interest and enhance their comprehension.

1. Examine the cover of the book. Ask students to predict the book's plot, characters, and setting.

2. Discuss the title. Ask students what they think *Kira-Kira* means, and see if they can predict anything about the book from its title.

3. Pose the following questions and ask students to respond:

   • What would it be like to lose a sister or brother?

   • What might it be like to move to a new town and school?

   • Would it be difficult to see your parents working all the time under poor conditions?

   • Why might students exclude another student from their friendships?

   • What do you know about Japan? Iowa? Georgia?

   • How important is your extended family to you?

   • What chores might you take on to help your parents?

   • What are your feelings about people of different ethnicities?

4. Direct students to work in groups or brainstorm what a new child in town might do to make friends. Share your suggestions with the class.

5. Direct students to work in groups to list the various countries their ancestors come from. This novel follows the life of a Japanese family who move from Iowa to Georgia.

6. Brainstorm the different ways in which students might help their parents, especially if both parents have to work. Think in terms of taking on chores and responsibilities, and also in terms of particular behaviors which can help parents.

7. Work in groups to discuss the illnesses of family and/or friends. Students may make a list of how they coped with their own and/or others' illness. This novel explores the serious illness of one main character. Students may want to examine their fears and beliefs about illness and death, previous to reading this novel.

About the Author

Cynthia Kadohata's grandparents married in Japan and immigrated in the 1920s to California to work as tenant farmers. Her father was interned in the Poston camp during World War II, before he was drafted and assigned to the U.S. Military Intelligence Service. Her mother, who lived in Hawaii at the time, was not interned.

When Cynthia was growing up, she wanted to be an astronaut. Unfortunately, she was prone to motion sickness. Once, she begged to get off a carnival ride before it had ended. The operator let her down, and she promptly collapsed, and then spent the rest of the night in the car!

Cynthia was born in Chicago, and lived in Georgia and Arkansas as a child. When she moved north, her accent was so strong that no one could understand her. For example, she called her sister Kim "Kee-uhm." Like Katie in *Kira-Kira*, Cynthia could easily eat five tacos at once as a child. Her record was six.

One of Cynthia's favorite books as a child was *The Diamond in the Window*, by Jane Langton. She met this author in a ladies' room one day and asked her for an autograph. The first story she herself wrote was all about a planet inhabited by one-legged ducks. Later, she earned her B.A. in Journalism from the University of Southern California. At twenty-five, she wasn't sure what she wanted to do with her life, so she took a Greyhound bus trip across the United States. Meeting new people and seeing new places inspired her to write. She began submitting short stories to magazines. She sent one story out every month, and about forty-eight stories later, *The New Yorker* published one.

Currently, Cynthia lives in the Los Angeles area near her brother. Her sister lives in Boston. Cynthia loves to travel throughout America. "Just thinking about the American landscape and focusing on it puts me in touch with what I think of as the real, essential me," she says on her website, **http://www.Kira-Kira.us.**

In 2004, Cynthia adopted a son from Kazakhstan, which is part of the former Soviet Union. She also owns a rescued purebred Doberman named Shika Kojika, which means "deer, little deer" in Japanese. Her other books include *The Glass Mountains, Floating World,* and *In the Heart of the Valley of Love.* Currently, Cynthia is writing a book about a friendship between a Japanese-American girl living in a World War II internment camp, and a boy on a Mohave reservation.

Kira-Kira

By Cynthia Kadohata

(Atheneum, 2004)

Katie and her older sister Lynn move with their family from Iowa to Georgia so that their parents can go to work in a chicken hatchery. Once there, the girls go to school, where they experience racism because they are Japanese.

Eventually, Lynn makes a friend named Amber. Katie and Lynn get a new baby brother, Sam.

Then, Lynn begins to get sick a great deal of the time. Apparently, she has anemia, which makes her tired. Katie's parents work overtime at the chicken hatchery. Katie accompanies her mother one day and meets a girl named Silly Kilgore. Silly tells her that the workers in the hatchery are trying to form a union so that they have more rights, such as taking bathroom breaks. Katie's mother won't join the union, however, as she's afraid of losing her job.

Lynn has to go to the hospital. Uncle Katsuhisa and Aunt Fumi stay with Katie and Sam, and they grow sad after a phone call from the hospital. Then, Katie's parents announce that they are buying a house.

In the new house, Lynn begins to get better. She and Katie and Sam go on a picnic, and Sam gets his foot caught in a trap. Katie runs for help and meets Hank Garvin, a friendly man who doesn't show any racism. Soon after, Lynn gets sick again and she and Katie get into an argument. Shortly thereafter, Uncle Katsuhisa and Aunt Fumi take Katie and Sam camping. Then, Katie learns that Lynn has lymphoma and might die.

Lynn grows weaker. She asks Katie to promise to take care of their family. On New Year's Day, Lynn passes away. Katie's family is devastated. Her father attacks his employer's private property. Her parents work all the time, and barely eat or sleep. Katie struggles to improve her grades and take care of her family. Then, her father takes them to California—a place that Lynn had hoped to visit. There beside the ocean, Katie realizes her sister will always be with her.

Vocabulary Lists

Below are lists of vocabulary words for each section of chapters in Kira-Kira. The following page offers ideas for using this vocabulary in classroom activities.

Section 1 (Chapters 1–3)

poultry	floozy(ies)
hatchery	placid
unruffled	femininity
variation	annoyance
madman	geyser
hysterics	
kimono	
constellation	

Section 2 (Chapters 4–6)

homecoming	shun(ned)
queen	disdain
sultry	stealth(ily)
capitalistic	lollygagging
enterprise	chasm
meld	hysterical
chiffon	
chronicle(d)	
consistent	
fatigue	

Section 3 (Chapters 7–9)

azalea	anemic
heyday	corroded
Seminole	theme
murky	humble
morbid	wrath
thug	boisterous
muggy	melodramatic
exasperated	

Section 4 (Chapters 10–12)

vague	unabashed(ly)
heathen	idiotic
alcove	exhilarated
magnolia	profusely
commotion	pallor
apprehensive	incubator
gurney	ritual
descent	

Section 5 (Chapters 13–15)

mournful	surreal	altar
traction	maggots	injustice
recede	dogged(ly)	
radioactive	implied	
dispute	urn	
Incan	Buddhist	
frenzy		

8

Vocabulary Activity Ideas

You can help your students learn the vocabulary words in *Kira-Kira* by providing them with the stimulating vocabulary activities below.

1. Ask students to work in groups to create an **Illustrated Book** of the vocabulary words and their meanings.

2. Group students. Direct groups to use vocabulary words to create **Crossword Puzzles** and **Word Searches.** Groups can trade puzzles with each other and complete, then check each other's work.

3. Play **Guess the Definition**. One student writes down the correct definition of the vocabulary word. The others write down false definitions, close enough to the original definition that their classmates might be fooled. Read all definitions, and then challenge students to guess the correct one. The students whose definitions mislead their classmates get a point for each student fooled.

    Use the word in five different sentences. Compare sentences and discuss.

4. Write a **Short Story** using as many of the words as possible. Students may then read their stories in groups.

5. Encourage your students to use each new vocabulary word in a **Conversation** five times during one day. They can take notes on how and when the word was used, and then share their experiences with the class.

6. Play **Vocabulary Charades**. Each student or group of students gets a word to act out. Other students must guess the word.

7. Play **Vocabulary Pictures**. Each student or group of students must draw a picture representing a word on the chalkboard or on paper. Other students must guess the word.

8. Challenge students to a **Vocabulary Bee**. In groups or separately, students must spell the word correctly, then give its proper definition.

9. Talk about **Parts of Speech** by discussing the different forms that a word may take. For instance, some words may function as nouns, as well as verbs. The word "fatigue" is a good example of a word which can be both a noun and a verb. Some words which look alike may have completely different meanings; in *Kira-Kira*, the word "constellation" is used to describe a particular named formation of stars, but it may also be used to describe a group of people or objects.

10. Ask your students to make **Flash Cards** with the word printed on one side and the definition printed on the other. Ask your students to work with a younger class to help them learn the definitions of the new words, using the flash cards.

11. Create **Word Art** by writing the words with glue on stiff paper, and then covering the glue with glitter or sand. Alternatively, students may write the words with a squeeze bottle full of jam on bread to create an edible lesson!

Quiz Time

Answer the following questions about Chapters 1–3.

1. Why does Lynn write that Katie saved her life? _____

   _____

   _____

2. Why do Katie's parents decide to move to Georgia? _____

   _____

   _____

3. What are the differences between Katie's father and Uncle Katsuhisa? _____

   _____

   _____

4. Why is Katie sad to leave Iowa? _____

   _____

   _____

5. Why does the woman at the hotel give Katie's family a back room and charge them extra money?

   _____

   _____

6. What does Katie notice about white people in Georgia? _____

   _____

   _____

7. What do the farm kids understand about death, according to Uncle Katsuhisa? _____

   _____

   _____

8. Why does Katie miss her parents at the end of Chapter 3? _____

   _____

   _____

Making Rice Balls

"Rice balls are called *onigiri*, and they were the only thing I knew how to make. To make *onigiri*, you wash your hands and cover your palms with salt. Then you grab a handful of rice and shape it into a lump."

—*Kira-Kira*

Japanese people often eat *onigiri* for lunch or snacks. With fillings such as salmon or pickled plums, rice balls become a sandwich!

Note: Please check for allergies before using this recipe.

Onigiri

Ingredients

- 10 cups uncooked white or Japanese-style rice
- salt
- package of toasted sesame seeds
- bottle of soy sauce

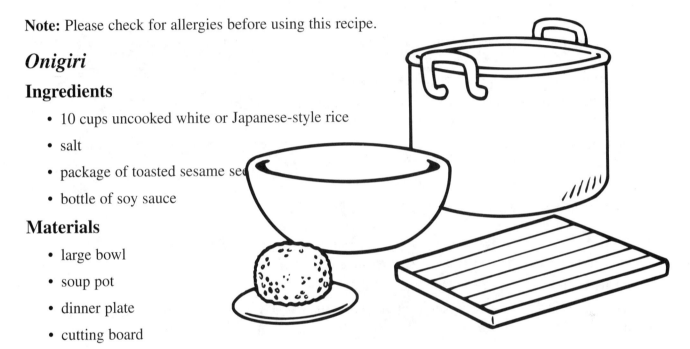

Materials

- large bowl
- soup pot
- dinner plate
- cutting board

Directions

1. Place the rice in a bowl and rinse with cold water until the water runs clear.

2. Put the rinsed rice in the soup pot with five quarts of cold water and bring to a gentle boil.

3. Turn down the heat, cover the pot, and simmer for 20-30 minutes until the rice is sticky. In the meantime, sprinkle a plate with salt.

4. When the rice has cooked, wet your palms and cover them lightly with salt. Shape a handful of rice into a ball or triangle. Roll ball in sesame seeds and enjoy!

Serves 24

Variation: Try making rice balls with chopped up vegetables such as cucumbers or thinly-sliced carrots, bits of scrambled eggs, or shredded canned salmon.

Playing Chess

Uncle Katsuhisa is dismayed when Lynn wins each of their chess games. He buys a marble chess set on the way to Georgia and challenges Lynn to another game. Once again, she wins.

Chess requires two players. Each player moves one set of pieces, one set white and the other black. First, place your pieces on the board like this:

There are six types of pieces. Each moves in a different way.

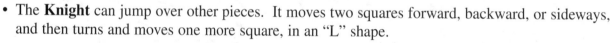
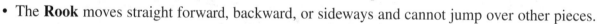

- The **Pawn** has two different moves. It can either move to the empty square directly in front of it, or move to capture a piece diagonally frontward on the left or on the right. Remember: On a pawn's first move, it may move two squares straight ahead, but it can't jump over another piece.
- The **King** moves one square in any direction, but don't move him to a square where he could be captured by your opponent!
- The **Queen** moves in a straight line in any direction. She can capture pieces, but she can't jump over them.
- The **Bishop** can only move diagonally, and cannot jump over other pieces.
- The **Knight** can jump over other pieces. It moves two squares forward, backward, or sideways, and then turns and moves one more square, in an "L" shape.
- The **Rook** moves straight forward, backward, or sideways and cannot jump over other pieces.

The Goal of the Game: Your goal is to capture your opponent's King. Move pieces strategically, capturing your opponent's other pieces so that he/she has less ability to defend the King.

How to Begin: The first player moves one of his/her pieces from its current square on the board to another square. The square it moves to must either be empty, or occupied by an opponent's piece. If the square contains the opponent's piece, the piece is removed from the board. This is called "capturing."

How to Conclude: When you make a move that puts your opponent's King in danger of being captured, say "Check." This gives your opponent a chance to make a move protecting his/her King. If no move is possible, you say "Checkmate." This means that you can capture the King and win!

Bishop   Queen   Rook   King   Pawn   Knight

The 1950s

As Katie travels with her family, she notices strange things. For instance, the woman at the hotel makes her family stay in a back room. Restaurants in Georgia have signs saying "Colored in Back." There are only 31 Japanese people living in Katie's new town of Chesterfield.

Break into groups of three or four. Using encyclopedias, books, and the Internet, answer the questions below to explore history and society in the United States during the 1950s.

1.

   a. What was Japanese Internment? _____

      _____

   b. When did it take place? _____

      _____

   c. How might this have affected the way Katie and her family were treated by others? _____

      _____

2.

   a. What was the Civil Rights movement? _____

      _____

   b. When did it take place? _____

      _____

   c. Why do you think Katie sees only white people sitting at the front of restaurants in Georgia?

      _____

3.

   a. What was the Civil War? _____

      _____

   b. When did it take place? _____

      _____

   c. How might Georgia be affected by the Civil War during the 1950s? _____

      _____

4.

   a. What is racism? _____

      _____

   b. What examples of racism does Katie observe in Section 1 of *Kira-Kira*? _____

      _____

Keeping a Diary

Lynn keeps a diary, and uses it to record the exciting and important events in her life. A diary doesn't have to be expensive—it can be a small notebook which you write in as often as you wish. You might even choose to add illustrations and photographs.

Begin a page in your diary by answering, in detail, the question below. Add illustrations to enhance your writing.

Write about a time that someone rescued you from danger. Use specific details to bring this experience to life!

Quiz

Answer the following questions about Chapters 4–6.

1. Why do Lynn and Katie save their nickels instead of spending them?

   _____

   _____

2. According to Lynn, why might some people at school ignore Katie?

   _____

   _____

3. What three things does Lynn want most in the world?

   _____

   _____

4. What happens to Lynn after the boy hits her with the ball?

   _____

   _____

5. How does Lynn change after she meets Amber?

   _____

   _____

6. How does Lynn hurt Katie's feelings?

   _____

   _____

7. Why does Uncle Katsuhisa take the children camping?

   _____

   _____

8. Why don't Katie's parents go on the camping trip?

   _____

   _____

Short Story

"Sometimes, in case she became a famous writer, Lynn practiced writing little stories in her diary . . ."

—*Kira-Kira*

Lynn writes a short story about a witch who casts a spell on the world's creatures. The flying animals could suddenly walk, and the walking animals could suddenly fly.

On the page below, write a short story of your own. The phrase, "suddenly, everything changed" must appear somewhere in your story! Have fun, and be creative!

Once upon a time . . . _____

_____

_____

_____

_____

_____

_____

_____

_____

_____

_____

_____

_____

_____

_____

_____

_____

Going Camping

Lynn and Amber persuade Uncle Katsuhisa to take them camping one weekend. Using encyclopedias, books, and the Internet, research the answers to the following questions in groups of three or four.

1. What national scenic trail runs through Georgia, all the way up to Maine?

   _____

   _____

2. What is the Trail of Tears National Historic Trail in Georgia?

   _____

   _____

   _____

Now, choose one of the following topics to research. Then, write a short skit demonstrating how to complete the task you've chosen. Feel free to make it funny and creative! Perform your skit for your classmates.

1. How should you make and put out a safe campfire?

2. What steps should you take to make sure that wild animals don't eat your food while you're camping?

3. How do you make the popular camping dessert called "S'mores"?

4. What should you do if you're bitten by a poisonous snake in the wilderness?

Dodgeball

Katie and Lynn and the other kids from the apartments play dodgeball after school. One little boy doesn't understand the rules, and so he accidentally hits Lynn in the chest with the ball.

Dodgeball is a popular sport. There is even an International Dodgeball Federation! You can play dodgeball with your classmates, remembering to <u>roll</u> the ball <u>gently</u> toward their feet.

Materials

- a rubber playground ball, about 14" in diameter

- sidewalk chalk

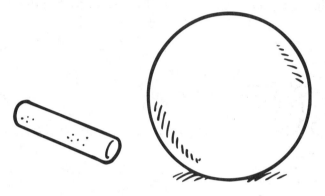

Directions

1. Draw a large circle on the school playground with sidewalk chalk. Count off into two teams.

2. The first team positions itself inside the circle, in various spots. The second team arranges itself around the outside of the circle. The person with the closest birthday holds the ball and starts the play.

3. The point of dodgeball is to <u>roll</u> the ball at the feet of classmates inside the circle. The children inside are allowed to run or jump away, but they must stay inside the circle.

4. If you throw the ball and it hits a classmate above the waist, you are disqualified from playing.

5. If you're inside the circle, and the ball touches you, you must become one of the players outside the circle.

6. The winner is the last person standing inside the circle!

Selfish and Unselfish Wishes

"Some nights before bed Lynn and I would make our wishes. First we made selfish wishes, and then we finished with unselfish wishes."

—*Kira-Kira*

What are your wishes? List them, according to the guidelines below.

1. What do you wish for yourself?

    a. _____

    b. _____

    c. _____

2. How can you help to make each wish for yourself come true?

    a. _____

    b. _____

    c. _____

3. What do you wish for others?

    a. _____

    b. _____

    c. _____

4. How can you help to make each wish for others come true?

    a. _____

    b. _____

    c. _____

Quiz Time

Answer the following questions about Chapters 7–9.

1. For what two reasons do the girls at school ignore Katie?

    _____

    _____

2. Why aren't employees allowed to gather in the parking lot of the poultry processing plant
    where Katie's mother works?

    _____

    _____

3. Why does Katie's mother tell her to "shut up"?

    _____

    _____

4. Why does Silly make Katie feel lazy?

    _____

    _____

5. Why isn't Katie's mother interested in joining the union?

    _____

    _____

6. Why does Lynn have to go to the hospital?

    _____

    _____

7. Why doesn't Katie know what to expect from Uncle Katsuhisa and Auntie Fumi when they
    come over?

    _____

    _____

8. Why do you think Auntie Fumi bursts into tears after the phone call?

    _____

    _____

The Ed Sullivan Show

On Katie's eleventh birthday, she gets to invite Silly to her house. The two girls sing and dance and pretend they're on the Ed Sullivan Show.

The Ed Sullivan Show was broadcast on television for over twenty years. The host, Ed Sullivan, invited rock stars, opera singers, ballet dancers, slapstick comics, literary writers, and many other talented guests to appear on his show.

You can hold a version of the Ed Sullivan Show in your classroom. First, choose one person to act as the moderator. He/she will introduce all acts to the audience. Now, form groups of three or four students. Each group will be responsible for a four-minute "act" in your class show. Acts can involve dance, instruments, readings, comic or serious skits, juggling, and any other talent your group wants to perform.

Each group should fill out the organizational form below.

Names of people in group: _____

_____

Title of act: _____

Description of act: _____

_____

Props needed:_____

_____

Costumes needed: _____

_____

Rehearsal days/times: _____

_____

Make sure to rehearse your act at least twice before performing it. As a class, choose a day and time for your show. Decide the order of acts by choosing a number out of a hat.

Consider inviting guests, such as other classes or parents, to watch your very own Ed Sullivan Show! Additionally, you may videotape the show to watch with popcorn at a later date.

● ● ● OOO   ▭   OOO

Unions

The workers at the chicken processing plant where Katie's mother works aren't allowed to use the bathroom during work. They aren't allowed to gather in the parking lot, either. Some of the workers, including Silly's mother, try to start a labor union. They hope to lobby for bathroom breaks and fair wages and hours.

In groups of three or four, use encyclopedias, books, and the Internet to answer the following questions about unions.

1. What is a labor union? _____

2. What was the Knights of Labor? _____

3. When was the American Federation of Labor established? _____

4. What were the goals of the American Federation of Labor? _____

5. Why was Mary Harris, otherwise known as Mother Jones, important to the development of labor unions? _____

6. What was the Triangle Factory Fire, and why was it important to the labor union movement?

   _____

   _____

7. Define the following words as they relate to labor unions:

   a. strike _____

   b. lockout _____

   c. boycott _____

   d. sweatshop _____

   e. mediator _____

   f. arbitrator _____

Now, the class will be divided into three groups. The first group will be employers. They are concerned about strikes and boycotts, and they're threatening a lockout.

The second group will be workers. They are concerned about long working hours with no breaks, low wages, and no overtime pay. They are threatening a strike and a boycott.

The third group will be mediators. They must find a way to make both employers and workers happy.

Stage a classroom debate, with employers on one side, workers on the other, and mediators in the front. Use specific examples to plead your case to mediators and attempt to negotiate so that everyone wins.

Playing Scrabble

An architect named Alfred Butts invented the game of Scrabble® in the 1930s, during the Great Depression. Scrabble uses a board of 225 (15 by 15) squares on which players form interlocking words using tiles printed with letters of the alphabet. Butts made a few sets to sell to friends. Then, in 1948, a man named James Brunot and his wife began making Scrabble games. They sold 2,000 sets in the first year, and then the owner of Macy's department store decided to stock the game! Today, there are versions of Scrabble in French, Dutch, Italian, Arabic, Russian, and Spanish.

Uncle Katsuhisa knows that Scrabble is a fun game which increases your knowledge of vocabulary words!

Materials

- Scrabble board and letters—one game for each group. Consider making your own!
- Dictionary—one for each group
- Paper and pencil

Directions

In groups of four, review the directions for Scrabble, below:

1. Put all letters in a bag. To decide who will start the game, each player chooses a tile. The person drawing a letter nearest to "A" begins.

2. Each player chooses seven tiles and places them on a rack so that other players can't see them.

3. The first player puts letters on the Scrabble board to make a word across or down, with one letter of the word on the board's "central square." Record the score on a piece of paper, along with double or triple scores for tiles placed on "premium squares." Note: A bonus of 50 points is awarded to a player who uses all seven tiles in one move!

4. The first player reaches into the bag and chooses enough tiles so that he/she has seven once again.

5. The player on the left must now add another word to the board, joining or interlocking with the first word on the board. The next player repeats this. All new words must use at least one of the letters that is already on the board.

6. **Notes**: Premium bonuses only apply the first time that letters are played. Also, instead of laying down a word, a player can exchange any number of tiles on their rack for new tiles from the bag. Scrabble includes two blank tiles which can represent any letters its player chooses. These can't be changed during the game.

7. The game ends when all tiles have been used and one player has laid down all his/her tiles. Players must deduct from their scores the value of unplayed letters. This total is added to the score of a player who has played all his/her tiles. The winner is the player with the highest score.

Sick!

In Section 3 of *Kira-Kira*, Lynn gets sick. The whole family is worried about her health.

Think about a time that you got sick. Using sensory details (that is, details that appeal to the reader's sense of smell, sight, touch, taste, and hearing), describe your illness in a page-long short story on a separate page. What did you feel like? How long did your illness last? Who took care of you? What did they do for you? Make sure to appeal to the five senses in your story.

Now, write down five actions you might take to appeal to a sick person's five senses, in order that he/she might feel better. Examples include playing quiet music, offering chicken soup, bringing the sick person a magazine, etc.

touch	
taste	
smell	
sight	
hearing	

Quiz Time

Answer the following questions about Chapters 10–12.

1. Why does Katie hit Amber? _____

   _____

   _____

2. Why do you think Lynn's parents buy her a house? _____

   _____

   _____

3. How does Katie feel about being alone?_____

   _____

   _____

4. What type of person is Hank Garvin? _____

   _____

   _____

5. How do Katie and Sam help the men in the chicken hatchery? _____

   _____

   _____

6. Why does Katie's father work constantly? _____

   _____

   _____

7. Why does Katie steal nail polish? _____

   _____

   _____

8. What does Katie discover about Lynn's illness?_____

   _____

   _____

Ocean Diorama

"As she always had been, Lynn was obsessed with the ocean, especially the ocean by
California. I read anything in the encyclopedia set we could think of that concerned
the ocean. She liked to know about everything, from the most peaceful tiny fish to the
hungriest shark."

> *—Kira-Kira*

You can make Lynn a diorama of the ocean. A diorama is a three-dimensional scene set against a
painted background.

Materials

- shoe box without a lid—your diorama
  will be inside it

- colored paper or paint

- glue

- scissors

- sand

- shells

- miniature items such as umbrellas, fish, crabs, towels, people, surfboards, and birds.

- crayons or markers

Directions

With colored paper or paint, you are going to create an ocean background for your diorama on the
inside of your shoebox.

1. Glue sand to the bottom inside panel to create a beach.

2. Now, glue miniature items inside your diorama to create an ocean scene. You might consider
   creating ocean waves and surfers out of colored paper, or making a deep-sea scene with replicas
   of sharks and whales. Consider hanging seagulls from the top inside of your shoebox and
   depicting sunbathers under umbrellas for a beach scene.

3. Write your name on the top of your box and display your diorama for everyone to enjoy!

Chickens

Both of Katie's parents work in the chicken business. What do you know about chickens? How much can you teach your classmates?

First, write each of the topics below on its own slip of paper. Form groups of three or four, and choose one slip of paper. This will be your group's topic. Use encyclopedias, books, and the Internet to find out as many interesting facts about your topic as you can. Fill out the Research Report below. Finally, share your findings with your classmates.

Topics

- Chicken Hatcheries
- Chickens as Pets
- Chicken Egg Farms
- Types of Chickens
- History of Chickens
- Famous Chickens in Books and Movies

Research Reports

Names of Students in Group: _____

_____

_____

Topic: _____

Short report on topic: _____

_____

_____

_____

_____

_____

_____

_____

_____

_____

Squares

Katie, Lynn, and Sam go on a picnic one summer afternoon. They play a game in which they each tell what they can see in an imaginary square. Lynn says, "Let's see how much we can see in the square. I'll go first. I see an ant."

For this project, you'll need to go outside, preferably into a field. Draw an imaginary square on the ground, about the length of a yardstick on all sides. Study it closely. A good observer remains very still and quiet so as not to disturb any living creatures within a location. Remember not to touch or damage anything in your square. Note: Even in paved areas, you can find plenty to observe, so look closely!

Now, draw what you've observed in your square in the space below. Color and label each item.

Themes

Katie has to write about the theme of *The Call of the Wild* for school. The theme of a novel refers to one idea that keeps coming up again and again in the story. In two paragraphs, below, explain the theme of *Kira-Kira*. You can use details from the book, as well as quotes, to support your observations. Here are suggestions for possible themes to get you started.

- family is important
- prejudice hurts people
- growing up can be difficult
- illness is hard on families

Quiz Time

Answer the following questions about chapters 13–15.

1. Why do Katie and Lynn have an argument? _____

   _____

2. Why is Katie glad to get out of her house over Thanksgiving? _____

   _____

   _____

3. Why can't Uncle Katsuhisa find work as a land surveyor? _____

   _____

4. What three things does Lynn ask Katie to promise she'll do? _____

   _____

   _____

5. Why does Katie's father break the windshield of Mr. Lyndon's car?_____

   _____

   _____

6. What does Katie find to be the main theme of Lynn's life? _____

   _____

   _____

7. How does Mr. Lyndon react when Katie's father apologizes? _____

   _____

   _____

8. Do you think Katie's mother joins the union? Why/why not?_____

   _____

   _____

Constellations

Lynn, Katie, and Sam love to go outside and look at the stars in the night sky. Constellations are formations of stars viewed as a design—there are 88 constellations based on classical mythology, animals, and objects.

You can create your own constellation indoors!

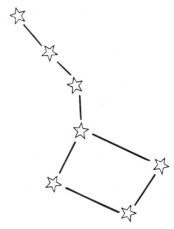

Materials

- books, encyclopedias, or the Internet
- one piece of black construction paper, 8½" x 11"
- one piece of white construction paper, 8½" x 11"
- a hole puncher
- glue
- thumbtacks
- one file card
- pencil

Directions:

1. First, research constellations using books, encyclopedias, or the Internet. Choose your favorite constellation. Neatly write down its name and description on your file card.

2. With the pencil, draw on the piece of black paper a small circle for each of the stars that make up your constellation. Using the hole puncher, punch holes where you drew the circles.

3. Now, glue the white paper behind the black paper. The white paper "shines" through so that everyone can see your constellation! Tack your project to the bulletin board with the file card directly below, so that classmates can read about your discovery.

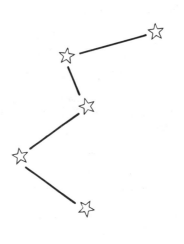

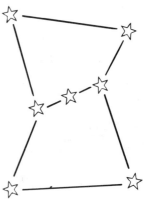

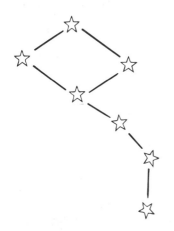

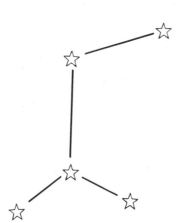

Do You Hear What I Hear?

On New Year's Day, Katie sits in the empty lot on the corner of her street. She lists the sounds that she hears: the flutter of a newspaper, a mechanical whirring, the chirp of a bird, and the click of a bug light.

How many sounds can you hear in three minutes? Choose a partner, and find out!

Materials

- a wristwatch or clock
- two pieces of paper
- two pencils or pens

Directions

You may choose to complete this assignment in one of two ways. First, choose a location with your partner, indoors or out. For three minutes, listen quietly to identify as many sounds as possible. Consider closing your eyes to block out distractions. At the end of three minutes, write down a list of all the sounds that you heard. Compare lists with your partner.

Alternatively, you can take turns with your partner, leading him/her blindfolded around a chosen space for three minutes, and then letting your partner record the sounds that he/she heard. When you've each had a turn, compare lists with your partner.

Finally, share your list with the class. On the board, tally up sounds heard most frequently, and least frequently.

Traveling through the United States

Katie travels with her family from Iowa to Georgia, and then to California. Illustrate the map on page 38 to show her travel route.

Materials

- 8½" x 11" map of the United States (see page 38)
- crayons or markers
- stickers or colored paper
- glue
- miniature objects such as leaves, toy chickens, shells, etc.

Directions

- First, draw the route Katie and her family took from Iowa to Georgia. Reread parts of section 1 to make sure you draw the correct route.
- Now, draw the route the family might have taken to California.
- Finally, draw pictures on your map to illustrate what Katie and her family might have seen on their journey. You might draw the five-story building Katie sees in St. Louis, or the crows she notices in California. Review the book to remind yourself of all that Katie observes on her travels.

Using an encyclopedia, atlas, or the Internet, answer the following questions:

1. How many miles are there between Iowa and Georgia? _____

2. If Katie's family drives an average of 60 miles per hour, how many hours does it take them to make this trip? _____

3. How many miles are there between Georgia and California? _____

4. How many hours does it take them to make this trip, if they drive an average of 60 miles per hour? _____

5. How many states does Katie's family cross if they drive in a straight line between the capital city of Georgia and the capital city of California? _____

_____

Five Stages of Grief

A woman named Dr. Elisabeth Kübler-Ross developed a guide to the grieving process a person goes through after someone becomes ill, and then dies. The five stages are:

1. Denial
2. Anger
3. Bargaining
4. Depression
5. Acceptance

Read back through *Kira-Kira* to see how Katie and her family move through the various stages of grief after Lynn gets sick. Describe their behavior as it relates to each stage below. The first one has been done for you.

Denial: The family says that Lynn just has anemia. They buy her a house, believing that this will make her lymphoma go away.

Anger: _____

_____

Bargaining: _____

_____

Depression: _____

_____

Acceptance: _____

_____

Has someone close to you (a friend, a relative, a pet) gotten very sick, or died? Describe your own experience of grieving. Did your reaction to this incident show any of the five stages of grief?

_____

_____

_____

_____

Any Questions?

When you finished reading Kira-Kira, did you have questions that were left unanswered? Write some of your questions here.

1. _____

2. _____

3. _____

4. _____

5. _____

Work in groups or by yourself to predict possible answers for some or all of the questions you asked above, as well as those written below. When you have finished, share your predictions with your class.

Does Katie go to college? _____

Does she move to California?_____

Does Katie's family stay in the chicken business?_____

Does Uncle Katsuhisa become a land surveyor? _____

Do Katie's parents become active union members? _____

Do Katie and Silly remain best friends?_____

Does Katie ever steal again? _____

Do Katie's parents stay in Georgia? _____

Does Katie ever see Hank Garvin again? _____

Does Katie forget Lynn?_____

Does the hatchery begin to allow employees to take bathroom breaks? _____

Does Katie begin to get good grades? _____

Does Mr. Lyndon make Katie's father pay for the damage to his car? _____

Does Katie experience prejudice at her high school? _____

Does Katie get a boyfriend? _____

What happens to Sam? _____

What does Katie become when she grows up? _____

Book Report Ideas

There are several ways to report on a book after you have read it. When you have finished *Kira-Kira,* choose a method of reporting from the list below, or come up with your own idea on how best to report on this book.

Make a Book Jacket

Design a book jacket for this book. On the front, draw a picture that you feel best captures this story. On the back, write a paragraph or two which summarizes the main points of this book.

Make a Time Line

On paper, create a time line to show the significant events in Katie's or Lynn's life. You may illustrate your timeline, if you wish.

Design a Scrapbook

Use magazine pictures, photographs, and other illustrations to create a scrapbook that Katie might keep to document life with her family. She might choose to decorate her scrapbook with sketches of birds, trees, or the towns he sees as they move from Iowa to Georgia. She might paste photos of Lynn and Sam, or chicken feathers, or lyrics to songs by the Shirondas into the book.

Make a Collage

Using old magazines and photographs, design a collage that illustrates all of Katie's adventures in the novel.

Create a Time Capsule

What items might Katie put in a time capsule by which to remember Lynn? What container might she use as a time capsule?

Write a Biography

Do research to find out about the life of author Cynthia Kadohata. You may use the Internet (Cynthia has her own website at **http://www.Kira-Kira.us/**) or magazines. Write a biography, showing how Cynthia's experiences might have influenced *Kira-Kira.*

Act Out a Play

With one or two other students, write a play featuring some of the characters in this novel. Then act out your play for your class.

Design a Diorama

Using a shoebox as a frame, create a diorama that illustrates an important scene in the novel. You may use all sorts of materials (paper, sand, clay, paint, fabric, etc.) to bring this scene to life.

Make Puppets

Using a variety of materials, design puppets to represent one or all of the characters in *Kira-Kira.* You may decide to work with other students to write and perform a puppet show.

Research Ideas

As you read *Kira-Kira*, you discovered geographical locations, events, and people about which you might wish to know more. To increase your understanding of the characters, places, and events in this novel, do research to find additional information.

Work alone or in groups to discover more about one or several of the items listed below. You may use books, magazines, encyclopedias, and the internet to do research. Afterwards, share your findings with the class.

- Iowa
- Georgia
- California beaches
- chicken hatcheries
- lymphoma
- The Ainu people of Japan
- Japanese celebrations
- Japanese racism in the 1950s
- Japanese internment during World War II
- The Ed Sullivan Show
- The Shirondas
- astronomy
- chess
- The Civil War
- Antebellum mansions
- nuclear bomb tests
- labor unions
- Japanese mourning rituals
- grief
- anemia
- *The Call of the Wild*
- The Twilight Zone
- The Seminole Indians
- bows and arrows
- Chesterfield, Georgia
- famous diaries
- magnolia trees
- the ocean
- Santa Ana winds
- crows

Map of the United States

Use this map with the activity on page 33.

Japanese Celebration

"New Year's is the biggest holiday of the year for the Japanese. Every year since we'd lived in Georgia, Mrs. Muramoto held a big party. She served *sake* and *mochi* and a couple dozen different snacks."

—Kira-Kira

Plan a Japanese celebration in your classroom. Consider inviting guests—another class, or your family members, to join in this celebration.

Party Checklist

Three weeks before the party . . .

❏ Decide when and where the party will occur.

❏ Discuss how to work a Japanese theme in to your party. Will you dress in traditional Japanese clothing, play chess or Japanese games, and eat Japanese food? Perhaps you'll play Japanese music and include a short Power-Point presentation on Japan.

❏ Decide whether your class wants to invite guests to the party. If so, make and send invitations.

❏ Discuss decorations. Many Japanese people are skilled in the art of origami. Consider making origami cranes and other objects, as they appear on page 40 of this book.

Two weeks before the party . . .

❏ Decide what food/drink you will make as a class. This book provides recipes for rice balls and mochi. Hot tea would also be appropriate.

❏ Pass around a sign-up sheet. Each student should be encouraged to bring something unique to the party. They might bring food, sign up to play musical instruments, bring a favorite song or object for show and tell, or show off a skill such as juggling or gymnastics.

❏ Send home a note to students' parents to let them know the day/date of the party, as well as what the student signed up to bring.

One week before the party . . .

❏ Send home a note reminding students of what they are to bring for the party.

❏ Buy and/or make decorations.

The day before the party . . .

❏ Make rice balls and mochi.

The day of the party . . .

❏ Decorate the party space.

❏ Make tempura vegetables and hot tea.

❏ Put on Japanese music.

Enjoy!

A Thousand Cranes

The crane is the unofficial national bird of Japan. For centuries, people have believed that if you fold a thousand origami cranes, your wish will be heard. Origami is the ancient Japanese art of paper-folding. You probably won't want to fold a thousand cranes, but consider folding several as a class to use as decorations for your Japanese celebration.

Materials

- Per student, one square, at least 6" x 6", of origami paper or thin-stock colored paper.

Directions

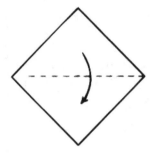

1. Fold paper in half diagonally, as shown here.

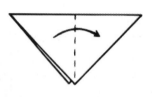

2. Fold paper in half to make a smaller triangle.

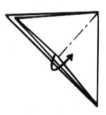

3. Spread the pocket out from the inside, as shown on figure 3. Fold to make a square.

4. Turn the paper over.

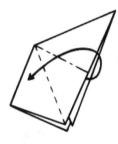

5. Repeat step 3.

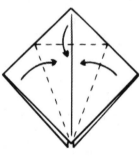

6. Fold left and right corners toward the center line. Then fold top corner. These folds create a crease.

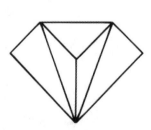

7. Your figure should look like this.

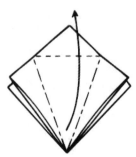

8. Now, pull the bottom corner up and fold inward.

9. Your figure should look like this. Turn the paper over and repeat steps 6, 7, and 8.

A Thousand Cranes *(cont.)*

10. Your figure should look like this.

11. Fold top layer as shown here.

12. Your figure should look like this. Turn paper over.

13. Repeat step 11 on this side.

14. Reverse fold as shownhere.

15. Form the crane's head by opening up the side and folding up the head.

16. Repeat steps 14 and 15 to form the crane's tail, as shown here.

17. Reverse fold to form a beak, as long as you'd like!

18. Bend wings into position, as shown here.

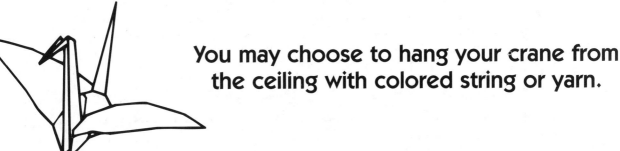

You may choose to hang your crane from the ceiling with colored string or yarn.

Mochi

Katie's family enjoys mochi at their celebrations. Mochi is a soft, chewy Japanese dessert.

(makes 36 servings)

Note: Please check for allergies before using this recipe.

Ingredients

- 1 pound mochiko (glutinous rice flour, available at Asian markets)
- 2½ cups white sugar
- 1 t. baking powder
- 2 cups water
- 1 t. vanilla extract
- 1 14-ounce can coconut milk
- ¼ t. red food coloring, or another color, if you prefer
- 1½ cups potato starch

Materials

- 9 x 13-inch pan
- wooden or stainless steel spoon
- medium and large bowls
- foil
- plastic knife (Mochi doesn't stick as much to plastic.)

Directions

1. Preheat oven to 350° F (175° C). Grease a 9 x 13-inch pan.

2. Stir together the rice flour, sugar, and baking powder in a large bowl.

3. In a medium bowl, mix water, vanilla, coconut milk, and red food coloring. Blend this into the rice flour mixture. Pour into greased pan.

4. Cover the pan with foil and bake for one hour.

5. Allow the mochi to cool completely, then turn it out onto a clean surface that has been dusted with potato starch. Cut into bite-sized pieces with a plastic knife.

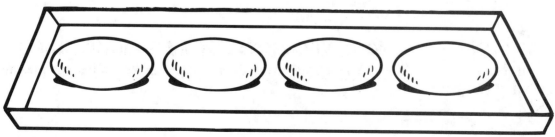

Objective Test and Essay

Matching: Match the descriptions of the characters with their names.

   1. Katie
   2. Lynn
   3. Uncle Katsuhisa
   4. Aunt Fumi
   5. Katie's mother
   6. Katie's father
   7. Silly Kilgore
   8. Sam
   9. Amber
   10. Mr. Lyndon

   a. gets depressed when he can't beat Lynn at chess
   b. isn't allowed to take bathroom breaks at work
   c. is Lynn's best friend at school for a while
   d. ate five tacos after a tragedy
   e. gets his foot stuck in a trap
   f. persuades Uncle Katsuhisa to let Amber shoot an arrow
   g. lives in a mansion in Georgia
   h. loves to imitate the Shirondas with Katie
   i. makes Katie promise to get good grades and go to college
   j. smashes Mr. Lyndon's car windshield to pieces

True or False: Answer true or false in the blanks below.

_____1. Katie's family moves to Georgia because they don't like Iowa.

_____2. Everyone at school wants to be friends with Lynn and Katie.

_____3. Lynn always wins when she and Uncle Katsuhisa play chess.

_____4. Katie's parents don't work very hard.

_____5. Katie thinks about Lynn when she travels to California.

Short Answer: Write a brief response on separate paper.

   1. Why is Katie angry at Lynn?

   2. Why do Katie's parents work such long hours?

   3. How do people treat Katie and her family in Georgia?

   4. How is her family important to Katie?

Essay: Respond to the following on separate paper.

This is a book about how one family deals with illness and death. Each member deals with Lynn's lymphoma differently. Explain how each of them—Katie, her mother, her father, her aunt, her uncle—react to Lynn's illness and death.

Responding to Quotes

On separate paper, respond to the following quotes as selected by your teacher.

Chapter One: "If she hadn't saved my life first, I wouldn't have been able to save her life."

Chapter Three: "Uncle's cot was empty. I knew he was studying the chessboard."

Chapter Four: "Later that afternoon, when I didn't know an answer, my teacher looked disappointed and said, 'I've heard your sister is very smart.'"

Chapter Five: "Everything started to change the winter I was ten and a half. One unusually warm day in January all the kids from the apartments were playing dodgeball after school."

Chapter Six: "When they finished laughing, I realized they weren't laughing at me—they thought they were laughing with me."

Chapter Seven: "'He discourages union activity. He doesn't let any of the employees gather in the parking lot, even if they're not talking about the union.'"

Chapter Seven: "I decided that someday when I was rich, I was going to buy the factory and let the workers use the bathroom whenever they wanted."

Chapter Eight: "Silly needed to work to help pay for her school clothes. In her spare time she also helped her mother fold union flyers."

Chapter Nine: "She wanted a house, and she didn't care if she couldn't use the bathroom during work or if her fingers were so stiff that she couldn't move them when she got home."

Chapter Ten: "My sister got better every day, and I heard my mother telling my father that she thought the house itself was making Lynn better."

Chapter Eleven: "'Dad?' I said. 'Our bicycles are still out there. I'm sorry.'"

Chapter Twelve: "I stuck some beautiful pink polish in my pocket and walked calmly out."

Chapter Thirteen: "'We got a new house, and you're ruining everything!'"

Chapter Thirteen: "Inside the living room my father laid me on my cot. 'She's gone,' he said."

Chapter Fourteen: "The only thing I could think to say was, 'We're on our way to eat tacos!'"

Chapter Sixteen: "I was worried that if she saw me crying, she would be very unhappy and maybe she wouldn't be able to leave the earth the way she was supposed to."

44

Conversations

Work in groups according to the numbers in parentheses to act out the conversations that might have occurred in each of the following situations in *Kira-Kira*.

- Katie confesses to her parents that she's angry at Lynn for getting sick and dying. (3 people)

- Katie explains to her friend Silly that it's difficult to be Japanese in their town. (2 people)

- Lynn talks to Katie about what she hopes Katie will do with her life when she grows up. (2 people)

- Katie's mother talks to Silly's mother about joining the union. (2 people)

- Katie meets her imaginary boyfriend, Joe-John Abondondalarama. (2 people)

- Katie, Sam, and their parents have an oceanside ceremony for Lynn. (4 people)

- Mr. Lyndon's attorney confronts Katie's father about the destruction of the car. (2 people)

- Amber tells Lynn why she doesn't want to be her friend anymore. (2 people)

- Uncle Katsuhisa and Aunt Fumi talk about what it's like to be Japanese during the 1950s in Georgia. (2 people)

- Katie brings home her first "A" ever on a school paper and shows her parents. (3 people)

- Katie tells Silly all about her family's trip to the ocean. (2 people)

- Katie and Silly teach Sam to sing and dance with them for an upcoming talent show. (3 people)

- Katie's mother and other workers in the chicken factory demand better working conditions. (2 or more people)

- Katie returns to the store where she stole nail polish and explains her actions to the cashier. (2 people)

- Katie explains lymphoma to her classmates. (2 or more people)

- Katie's parents talk with Uncle Katsuhisa and Aunt Fumi about their jobs and lives. (4 people)

- Katie meets Hank Garvin again, and he asks about her sister. (2 people)

Bibliography of Related Reading

Fiction

Choldenko, Gennifer. *Al Capone Does My Shirts*. Putnam, 2004.

Coerr, Eleanor. *Sadako and the Thousand Paper Cranes*. Puffin Books, 1999.

Creech, Sharon. *Walk Two Moons*. Harper Trophy, 1994.

Denenberg, Barry. *The Journal of Ben Uchida*. Scholastic, 1999.

Garland, Sherry. *The Lotus Seed*. Voyager Books, 1997.

Halsey Anderson, Laurie. *Fever* 1793. Aladdin, 2002.

Henkes, Kevin. *Olive's Ocean*. Harper Trophy, 2005.

Lord, Betty Bao. *In the Year of the Boar and Jackie Robinson*. Harper Trophy, 1986.

Park, Linda Sue. *A Single Shard*. Clarion, 2001.

Paterson, Katherine. *Bridge to Terabithia*. Harper Trophy, 1987.

Shea, Pegi Deitz *Tangled Threads: A Hmong Girl's Story*. Clarion, 2003.C

Taylor, Mildred D. *The Land*. Phyllis Fogelman Books, 2001.

Non-Fiction

Birdseye, Debbie and Tom. *Under Our Skin: Kids Talk About Race*. Holiday House, 1997.

Heegaard, Marge. *When Someone Very Special Dies: Children Can Learn to Cope with Grief*. Woodland Press, 1988.

Houston, Jeanne and James. *Farewell to Manzanar: A True Story of Japanese American Experience During and After the World War II Internment*. Laurel Leaf, 1983.

Mofford, Juliet. *Talkin' Union: The American Labor Movement*. Sagebrush, 2001.

Morrison, Toni. *Remember: The Journey to School Integration*. Houghton Mifflin, 2004.

Mundy, Michaelene. *Sad Isn't Bad: A Good-Grief Guidebook for Kids Dealing with Loss*. Abbey Press, 1998.

Romain, Trevor. *What on Earth Do You Do When Someone Dies?* Free Spirit Publishing, 1999.

Stand Up for Your Rights. Two Can Publishers, 2000.

Web Sites

http://www.educationworld.com (Type in the search term *Labor Day*)

http://www.wikipedia.org (Type in the search terms *Labor Union, Japanese American Internment, five stages of grief, lymphoma*, etc.)

Answer Key

Page 10

1. Katie threw a milk bottle at the dog who was attacking Lynn, and he stopped to lap up the milk.
2. Katie's parents' store went out of business, and her uncle said he could get them a job at a chicken hatchery in Georgia.
3. Katie's father is quiet and serious, and he likes to read the newspaper. Uncle Katsuhisa is loud and jokes around a lot, and doesn't like the newspaper.
4. Katie loves her house in Iowa and doesn't want to move to an apartment in a town where people talk differently.
5. The woman is prejudiced; Katie and her family are Japanese, so she treats them poorly.
6. White people sit at the front of restaurants and touch her face as if they're not sure Katie is real.
7. The farm kids understand that death is a part of life.
8. Katie's parents work much more than they did in Iowa.

Page 13

1. Japanese Internment refers to the removal of approximately 112,000 to 120,000 Japanese Americans from their homes in the United States to housing facilities called "War Relocation Camps" after the Japanese bombing of Pearl Harbor in 1941. People in the U.S. may still have been suspicious of Japanese Americans in the 1950s, and thus, treated Katie and her family with prejudice.
2. The Civil Rights movement sought equal rights for African Americans during the 1950s, 1960s, and 1970s. Katie sees only white people sitting up front in Georgia restaurants because at the time, this area was segregated, and African Americans had to sit in the back.
3. The Civil War was fought in the U.S. from 1861 to 1865. Twenty-three northern states battled against the eleven southern states that had declared their secession from the U.S. in order to retain the practice of slavery. Less than a century later, racism still existed in the southern state of Georgia, extending not only to African Americans, but to the Japanese.
4. Racism is discrimination based on race. Katie notices the following: the woman at the motel charges her family extra for a back room; white people sit at the front of Georgia restaurants which have signs saying "Colored in Back"; white people come up to Katie and touch her face as if they're not sure she's real.

Page 15

1. Lynn and Katie save their nickels instead of spending them to help their parents buy a house.
2. According to Lynn, some people at school might ignore Katie because she is Japanese, and a minority at school.
3. Lynn wants to own a house, go to college, and live by the sea.
4. Lynn feels tired and complains that things "feel swirly." She sleeps through dinner.
5. Lynn begins to walk around with a book on her head, and experiments with makeup.
6. Lynn tells Katie she's not being ladylike, and that she won't be able to act like a child much longer.
7. Uncle Katsuhisa takes the children camping after Lynn and Amber beg him to because two boys from their school are camping as well.
8. Katie's parents don't go on the camping trip because they're exhausted from working so much.

Page 17

1. The Appalachian Trail.

2. The Trail of Tears National Historic Trail in Georgia commemorates the trail used by Cherokee American Indians who were forced to leave their homeland by the United States government.
a. After determining that fires are legal in your camping area, dig a fire ring of soil which is free of flammable material, to a depth of a few inches. Build your fire of tinder, kindling, and a log. Keep a hatchet and a bucket of water close by. Keep the fire small and free of sparks. To put out a fire, pour water on all the embers and stir the ashes until the sound of hissing has stopped. If water is scarce, sand may be used to smother the fire. Then, pour a small amount of water over the sand.
b. If you're car-camping, you should store all food, including toothpaste, in your car. If you're backpacking, you should put your food in animal-proof lockers if your camping site contains them. Never keep food in your tent!
c. The traditional S'more is made by roasting a marshmallow, then placing it between two graham crackers with a small square of chocolate.
d. If a poisonous snake bites you, stay calm. Do not try to suck out the poison by mouth. A suction device found in a basic snakebite kit may be placed over the bite to help draw venom out of the wound without making a cut. Wash the bite with soap and water, and immobilize the bitten area, keeping it lower than the heart. Get to a hospital as soon as possible. Students may also suggest calling 911 on a cell phone and carrying the victim out to a car or ambulance.

Page 20

1. The girls at school ignore Katie because she is Japanese, and because her mother works at a poultry plant.
2. Employees aren't allowed to gather in the parking lot because Mr. Lyndon is afraid they might start a labor union.
3. Katie's mother tells her to "shut up" because Katie says that Lynn looks gross.
4. Silly makes Katie feel lazy because she works to help pay for her school clothes and helps her mother fold union flyers.
5. Katie's mother isn't interested in joining the union because she's afraid she'll get fired and be unable to buy a house.
6. Lynn has to go to the hospital because she's so tired that she can't eat.
7. Katie doesn't know what to expect from Uncle Katsuhisa and Auntie Fumi when they come over because one day they'll fight, and the next day they'll be madly in love.
8. Students may guess that Auntie Fumi bursts into tears after the phone call because she's heard Lynn's diagnosis and knows it's bad.

Page 22

1. A labor union is an organization of employees created in order to bargain for fair labor practices with their employer.
2. The Knights of Labor was a secret organization that worked to maintain the rights of U.S. workers.
3. The American Federation of Labor was established in 1886.
4. The goals of the American Federation of Labor were to provide workers with shorter hours, safer working conditions, and fair pay.
5. Mary Harris, otherwise known as Mother Jones, was important to the development of labor unions because she helped to found the Industrial Workers of the World and worked as an organizer and educator in labor strikes around the world. She also helped to organize the wives and children of striking laborers. She was arrested for organizing a children's march,.

Answer Key *(cont.)*

6. The Triangle Factory Fire broke out in March 1911 at the Triangle Shirtwaist Factory, which was known to store flammable textiles and no fire extinguishers. More than one hundred mostly female workers died in the fire. It was important to the labor union movement because it inspired union activists to push for worker safety and worker compensation laws.

7. a. strike—when employees stop working in support of demands such as higher pay or improved conditions.

   b. lockout—when employers withhold work and close down a workplace during a labor dispute with employees.

   c. boycott—when consumers refuse to purchase a product in protest of an issue involved in the product's production.

   d. sweatshop—a shop or factory at which employees work long hours under poor conditions.

   e. mediator—a person who reconciles conflicts between employers and employees, non-legally.

   f. arbitrator—someone who legally settles issues between parties, such as employers and employees, who are engaged in a dispute.

Page 25

1. Katie hits Amber because she's stopped being friends with Lynn. Amber insults Katie's dress and calls her a heathen.

2. Students may guess that Lynn's parents buy her a house in hope that the purchase will improve their daughter's health.

3. Katie loves her brother and sister, and doesn't like to be alone.

4. Hank Garvin is kind and helpful and supportive.

5. Katie and Sam help the men in the chicken hatchery by bringing them coffee, scratching their backs, and lighting their cigarettes for them.

6. Katie's father works constantly because he has to pay the mortgage on their house and pay for Lynn's hospital bills.

7. Katie steals nail polish because Lynn wants some, and Katie doesn't have any money.

8. Katie discovers that Lynn has lymphoma and might die.

Page 30

1. Katie and Lynn argue because Lynn wants milk, and then water, and drops her cup on the floor.

2. Katie is glad to get out of her house over Thanksgiving because she needs time away from her parents.

3. Uncle Katsuhisa can't find work as a land surveyor because he's Japanese, and no one will hire him.

4. Lynn asks Katie to promise that she'll get better grades, go to college, and take care of their family.

5. Katie's father breaks the windshield of Mr. Lyndon's car for various reasons. He's angry about his daughter's death, angry at Mr. Lyndon's mistreatment of workers, and angry that he has to work constantly.

6. Lynn could take an everyday object and use it to demonstrate how amazing the world is.

7. Mr. Lyndon says that Katie's father will hear from his attorney about reimbursement for the damaged windshield.

8. Students will most likely guess that Katie's mother has joined the union, especially when they notice that she's pleased when the union wins a decision about "grief leave" by one vote.

Page 33

1. Iowa and Georgia are approximately 850 miles apart.

2. If Katie's family drives an average of 60 miles per hour, it will take them approximately 14 hours to make this trip.

3. Georgia is approximately 2,200 miles from California.

4. It will take them approximately 36.6 hours to make this trip, if they drive an average of 60 miles per hour.

5. If Katie's family drives in a straight line between the capital city of Georgia and the capital city of California, they cross nine states.

Page 34

Anger: Katie is angry at Lynn when she spills the milk. Katie's mother tells her to "shut up." Her father breaks Mr. Lyndon's car windshield.

Bargaining: Katie's parents buy Lynn a house, possibly bargaining that this will make her well.

Depression: The entire family cries. Katie's father may break Mr. Lyndon's windshield out of depression, as well. Her parents become "zombies" who talk about their regrets. They sleep little, and lose weight.

Acceptance: Katie's father visit's Lynn's grave and then takes the family to California for a vacation. Katie hears her sister's voice in the wind and reflects on how Lynn taught her that the world is magical.

Page 43

Matching

		True or False
1. d	6. j	1. False
2. i	7. h	2. False
3. a	8. e	3. True
4. f	9. c	4. False
5. b	10. g	5. True

Short Answer

1. Katie is angry at Lynn because she's sick, which causes their parents to have to work overtime. She's angry because her family is sick and tired all the time.

2. Katie's parents work such long hours to pay the mortgage and Lynn's hospital bills. They don't make much money in the chicken hatchery.

3. Most people don't treat Katie and her family well—there is evidence of racial prejudice against Japanese people in Georgia during this time. Hank Garvin and Silly Kilgore's mother are exceptions; they treat the family with respect.

4. Katie's family is extremely important. She loves being with them, and she looks to them for guidance and support.

Essay

Katie wants to help Lynn, and becomes frustrated and angry when she can't. She cries when Lynn dies, and tries to improve herself.

Katie's mother works overtime and grows increasingly short-tempered and sorrowful. She loses weight and sleeps little.

Katie's father also works overtime, and gets very quiet. He breaks Mr. Lyndon's windshield, and cries after Lynn dies. Finally, he visits her grave, then takes the family to California.

Aunt Fumi and Uncle Katsuhisa are sad when they hear of Lynn's illness, and they do all they can to support the family. They take Katie and Sam camping and play games with them.

Page 44

Grade students on comprehension of the story as evidenced by the length of answers and depth of responses.

Page 45

Grade students on comprehension of the story, knowledge of the characters, and creativity.